Tap Dancing
step•by•step

THOMAS SINIBALDI

Sterling Publishing Co., Inc. New York

Step shown in cover photo

Stand with your feet apart, knees slightly bent. Kick your left heel up to hit your right palm. The left foot crosses in front of your right leg. Return left foot to floor. Repeat using right foot and the palm of your left hand.

Cover photo shows author Thomas Sinibaldi with actress-model Geri Martin.

Thomas Sinibaldi modeled for his own book. Geri Martin, in the black leotard, is an actress in movies and on television. Carol Straker, in the white leotard, is a student of the author's.

Library of Congress Cataloging in Publication Data

Sinibaldi, Thomas.
    Tap dancing step by step.

    Includes index.
    1. Tap dancing.   I. Title.
GV1794.S55   793.3'24   81-50990
ISBN 0-8069-4656-3   AACR2
ISBN 0-8069-7556-3 (pbk.)
ISBN 0-8069-4657-1 (lib. bdg.)

Copyright © 1982 by Sterling Publishing Co., Inc.
Two Park Avenue, New York, N.Y. 10016
Distributed in Australia by Oak Tree Press Co., Ltd.
P.O.Box J34, Brickfield Hill, Sydney 2000, N.S.W.
Distributed in the United Kingdom by Blandford Press
Link House, West Street, Poole, Dorset BH15 1LL, England
Distributed in Canada by Oak Tree Press Ltd.
℅ Canadian Manda Group, 215 Lakeshore Boulevard East
Toronto, Ontario M5A 3W9
Manufactured in the United States of America
All rights reserved

The Fascination of Tap Dancing

Once you start tap dancing you will find it hard to stop. Once you make the very first tapping sounds with your feet you will become so excited that you will be spurred on to learn everything about tap dancing.

This book starts you off dancing in the very first lesson. And once that lesson is completed, you will feel the glow that comes with personal accomplishment.

Tap dancing is happy dancing. In watching Fred and Ginger gliding over Art Deco sets or Jimmy Cagney winging it down the stairs, one thing you notice is that they are smiling, and you will smile too. The popularity of tap is on the upswing again, with Broadway shows built around tap dancers like Ann Miller and Gregory Hines.

When you're tapping you're getting enjoyable exercise. You use your entire body, not just your feet and legs. You can even incorporate ballet movements into tap.

This book of 14 lessons starts you off with the basics of tap in easy-to-follow form. In just two weeks of daily lessons, you can learn all the basics and combinations. If you continue to practice much longer you might want to put on a performance with a group or by yourself. You might be able to master some techniques better than others. Don't try to learn everything at once. Just try to perfect one step or routine at a time.

How to Use This Book

Follow each lesson in order, exactly as it is written. Read it, dance it, read it again to be sure you are doing it correctly.

Dance at your own pace—usually try for an hour at a time unless that's more than enough for you. It's a matter of stamina.

Dance out one lesson per day if you can.

Don't dance when you are physically tired, and don't dance for two hours after you have eaten a heavy meal.

Repeat a lesson if you don't feel comfortable with the steps in the lesson or you haven't practiced for several days and have forgotten some of what you learned before.

Dancing involves repetition. The more effort and time you put into it, the better the quality of your step execution.

Dance with a partner if you find it helps you. Sometimes working with a dancer who is on the same learning level will be edifying for both of you.

Then, of course, you may want to take lessons at school or with a private teacher. In that case you can use the book as a supplement although it is written in such a way that you can learn all you need without a teacher.

Music

The sounds of tap are enhanced by proper music.

Measures

Music is divided up into many segments separated by a vertical line. These segments are called measures, and each measure has an equal number of beats or counts. That number depends on what is known as the music's time signature.

Time Signatures

For our purposes here we will discuss two types of time signatures: 3/4 and 4/4

3/4—The 3 tells us there are 3 counts per measure. 3/4 time is also called waltz time. "East Side/West Side" is a song in 3/4 time—Count 123, 123. . . .

4/4—The 4 tells us there are 4 counts per measure. 4/4 time is also called common time. "42nd Street" is a song in 4/4 time. Count 1234, 1234. . . .

Music for Tap Dancing

1. Any of the old standard songs will do.
2. Special instructional records may be ordered from music shops.

Recommendations

(The following music is in 4/4 time with the exception of "East Side/West Side" which is in 3/4 time.)

"Let Yourself Go"
"42nd Street"
"East Side/West Side"
"Hello, Dolly"
"One" (from *Chorus Line*)
"Slap That Bass"
"Stepping Out with My Baby"
"Tea for Two"
"Once in Love with Amy"

LPs = "Stepping Out"—Vicky Jo Boyer
"Tunes for Tap"—Danny Hoctor
"More Tunes for Tap"—Danny Hoctor
"Tap Happy"—Hoctor Records

Counting Music

You must know how to count out your steps before dancing with music.

Single, Double and Triple Time: If you tap your foot to a song in 4/4 time you would be tapping each beat out, 4 taps for each measure, 1234, 1234. This is called counting in single time, counting right on the beat.

In tap, we count two measures at a time. All this means is that instead of counting two measures in 4/4 time as 1234, 1234, you count two measures as 12345678.

Tapping your foot in single time means you tap a sound for each beat right on the beat.

If you were to count in double time you would count or tap *two* sounds for each beat, so two measures in 4/4 time would have sixteen counts or taps. One count is on the beat, the next count is in-between that beat and the next beat. That in-between beat is the "and" beat.

Counting two measures in 4/4 time would be counted

First Measure
1 and 2 and 3 and 4 and

Second Measure
5 and 6 and 7 and 8 and

or simply:

1 and 2 and 3 and 4 and 5 and 6 and 7 and 8 and. Sixteen counts with two counts for each beat.

If you were able to count in triple time you would count or tap three sounds for each beat. That would give you 24 counts or taps for each two measures. This third count is the "a" count.

Counting two measures in triple time would be counted

First Measure
1 and a 2 and a 3 and a 4 and a

Second Measure
5 and a 6 and a 7 and a 8 and a

or simply:
1 and a 2 and a 3 and a 4 and a 5 and a 6 and a 7 and a 8 and a

Summary

Single Time (One count for each beat)
  12345678
Double Time (Two counts for each beat)
  1 and 2 and 3 and 4 and 5 and 6 and 7 and 8 and
Triple Time (Three counts for each beat)
  1 and a 2 and a 3 and a 4 and a 5 and a 6 and a 7 and a 8 and a . . .

Shoes and Clothing

Illus. 1

Illus. 2

You will need tap shoes or metal taps attached to your dancing shoes. Herbet's, Selva and Capezio are some of the brand names you will find. Look in the commercial directory of your local phone book for shops catering to dancers. I myself prefer Capezio Teletone Taps.

Be sure the taps are screwed on tightly. They should stick out over the front of the toe and the back of the heel so that your taps with extended toe and heel will be heard.

To avoid sliding and slipping, have the shoe-maker glue a thin piece of rubber to your shoes between the front tap and the heel.

In Illus. 1 you can see how the taps and rubber should be attached.

Illus. 2 shows a good style of women's shoes.

As for clothing a man should wear a leotard and jazz pants or T-shirt and loose-fitting pants (Illus. 3) to allow freedom of movement.

A woman should wear a leotard and tights (Illus. 4) or loose-fitting pants and T-shirt to allow stretching and flexibility of body movements.

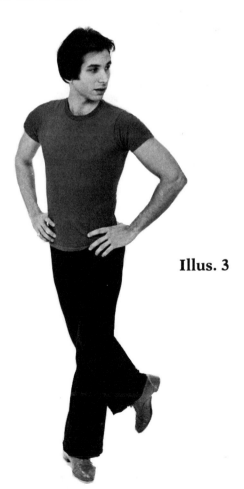

Illus. 3

Illus. 4

Illus. 5

Lesson One

Lesson One is divided into two parts. It is not necessary to practice both parts in one session. Should you care to try Part II on a different day, be sure to review Part I before you begin.

Illus. 6

This is a special kind of photograph which has been taken for some of the sequences—a "tracking" photo—so that you see in a single picture how your foot is supposed to move.

Lesson One-Part 1

Toe Tap

1. This sound is made by touching the floor with the toe tap on your shoe and lifting the tap off the ground by flexing your foot. (See Illus. 6.)

2. The action occurs by moving your foot at the ankle. Do *not* raise your leg up and down to tap the floor (Illus. 7, 8).

3. Your weight remains on the leg that is not tapping. We shall call that leg the *supporting* leg. The foot doing the tapping shall be called the *working* leg.

This step is done *en croix* ("on kwah") a ballet term meaning in a cross, derived from the shape of

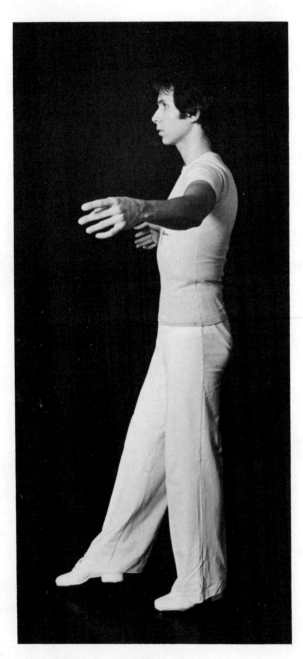

Illus. 7

Illus. 8

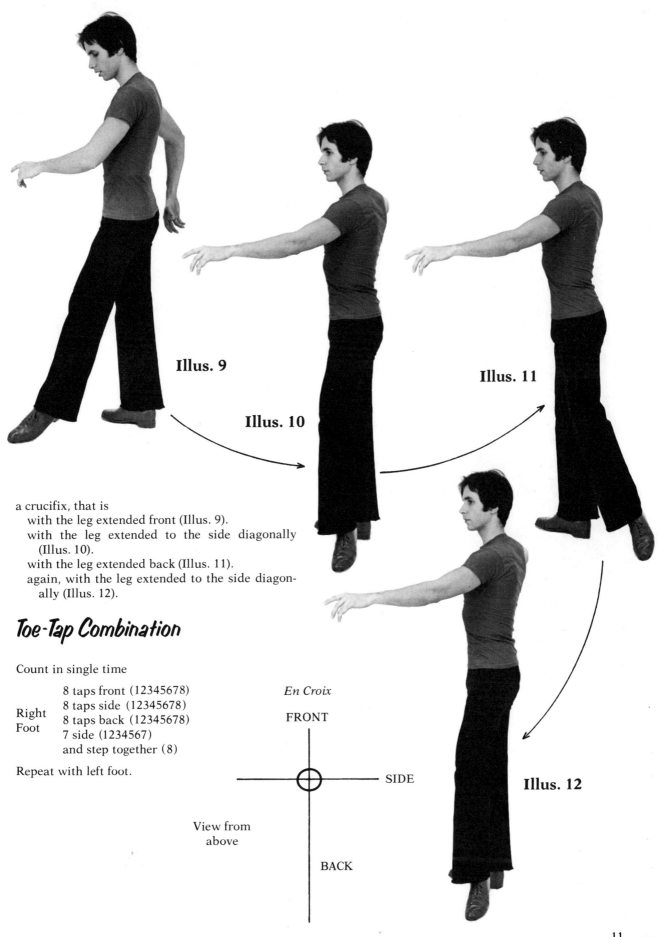

Illus. 9

Illus. 10

Illus. 11

a crucifix, that is
  with the leg extended front (Illus. 9).
  with the leg extended to the side diagonally
    (Illus. 10).
  with the leg extended back (Illus. 11).
  again, with the leg extended to the side diagon-
    ally (Illus. 12).

Toe-Tap Combination

Count in single time

<table>
<tr><td rowspan="5">Right
Foot</td><td>8 taps front (12345678)</td></tr>
<tr><td>8 taps side (12345678)</td></tr>
<tr><td>8 taps back (12345678)</td></tr>
<tr><td>7 side (1234567)</td></tr>
<tr><td>and step together (8)</td></tr>
</table>

Repeat with left foot.

En Croix

FRONT

SIDE

View from
above

BACK

Illus. 12

Illus. 14

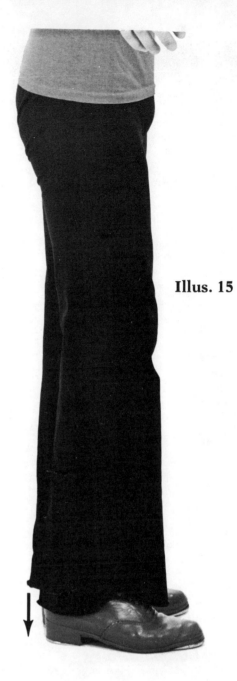

Illus. 15

Heel Drops

Feet slightly apart—this sound is made by lifting only your heel off the ground and dropping it back down in place (Illus. 14, 15).

Count in single time

8 heel drops with right foot (12345678)
8 heel drops with left foot (12345678)
16 heel drops alternating each foot
one right
one left, one right, etc.

Illus. 16

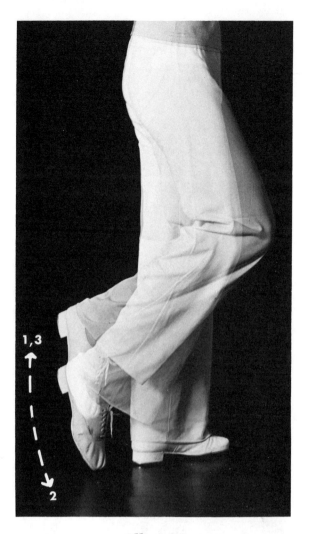

Illus. 17

Toe

1. This sound is made by hitting the floor behind you with the very tip of the toe tap and with your weight on the supporting or standing leg (Illus. 16).

2. Be sure to lift your toe off the ground once the sound is made (Illus. 17).

Count single time.

Right   Seven toes (1234567)
Foot   Step together next to left (8)
Repeat on left foot.

Now do:

Right foot   3 toes (123)
              step together (4)
Left foot   3 toes (567)
              step together (8)

Now do:

Right foot   1 toe   1
              step together 2
Left foot   1 toe   3
              step together 4
Right foot   1 toe   5
              step together 6
Left foot   1 toe   7
              step together 8

Illus. 18

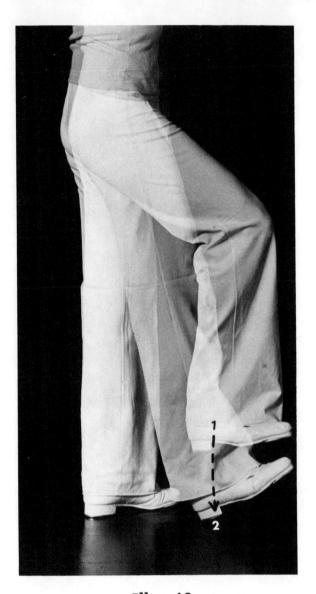

Illus. 19

Heel Digs

This sound is made by lifting the foot with a bent knee and tapping the back edge of the heel on the ground. Weight remains on the support leg. Illus. 18 shows knee up. Illus. 19 shows heel striking floor.

Count in single time

Right foot	3 digs (123)
	step next to left
	(together) (4)
Left foot	3 digs (567)
	step together (8)

Right foot	1 dig	1
	step together	2
Left foot	1 dig	3
	step together	4
Right foot	1 dig	5
	step together	6
Left foot	1 dig	7
	step together	8

Illus. 20

Illus. 21

Stamp

This sound is made by lifting your foot (Illus. 20) with knee bent (weight on supporting leg), and stamping the entire foot down on the ground. Transfer your weight to the stamping foot and lean forward, then step together. (Illus. 21).

Right foot	stamp	1
	step together	2
Left foot	stamp	3
	step together	4

Repeat this pattern 5678

Depending on how you feel, you may now go on to Part II of Lesson One. If you feel a little tired, take a break and continue this lesson later.

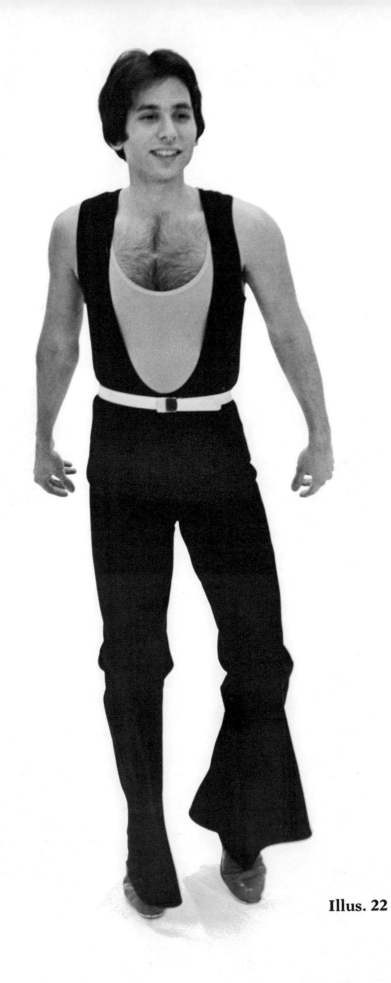

Illus. 22

Lesson One-Part II

Brush Front

1. This sound is made by brushing or striking the toe tap on the floor as the foot passes from back to front.

2. Start with your right foot raised toward the back (weight on left supporting leg) knee forward, slightly bent. *Brush*, trying to use only that part of your leg from the knee down (Illus. 23).

3. End with your foot slightly off the floor, leg straight (Illus. 24).

4. Be sure to brush the floor with the toe tap only, no heel.

Illus. 23

Illus. 24

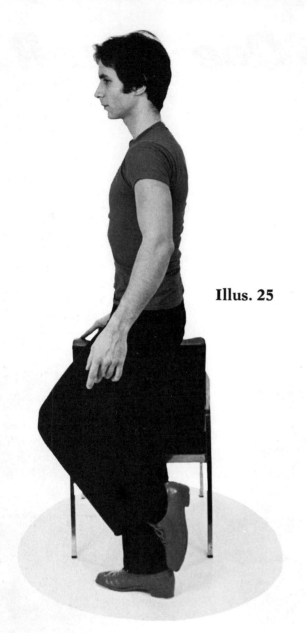

Illus. 25

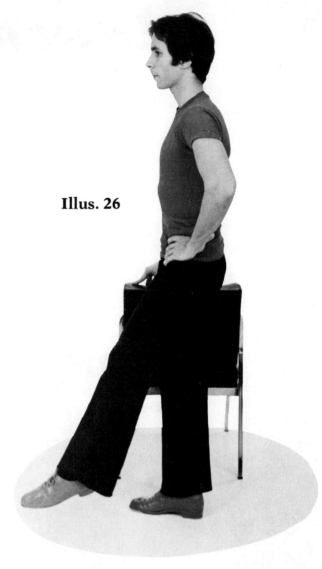

Illus. 26

Once you are able to balance comfortably, the chair will not be necessary.

5. This may be practiced while holding onto a chair (Illus. 25, 26).

Counting in single time:

	Counts
Begin with foot in starting position	
Brush front	1
Return foot to starting position	2

Do 16 brush fronts with your right foot holding the chair with your left hand at your left side.

To do this you will be counting from 1-8 4 times.

Do 16 brush fronts with your left foot holding the chair with your right hand at your right side (Illus. 25 and 26).

To do this you will be counting from 1-8 4 times.

Brush Back

1. This sound is made by brushing or striking your toe tap on the floor as your foot passes from front to back.

2. Start with your foot extended to the front, raised slightly off the floor (weight on supporting foot), knee straight, (Illus. 27) and *brush*, bending your knee, trying to use only that part of your leg from the knee down (Illus. 28).

3. End with your foot raised slightly off the floor in back of you, knee forward.

4. Be sure to brush the floor with your toe tap only, no heel.

5. This also may be done while holding onto a chair.

Do 16 brush backs on each foot in the same exact pattern as the brush front exercise you have just done.

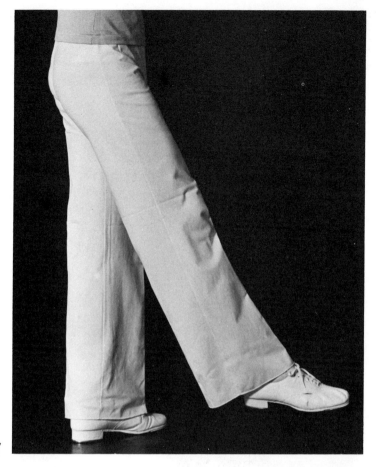

Illus. 27

Illus. 28

19

Tips on Balancing

1. Weight forward.

2. Knees bent.

3. Stomach in.

4. Back straight.

5. Bottom in.

6. If standing on left foot, right hip down.

7. If standing on right foot, left hip down.

Illus. 29

Shuffle

1. The shuffle has two sounds, a brush front and a brush back.

2. Combine the two previous steps (brush front and brush back) to make one shuffle.

3. Start (holding onto a chair, if necessary) with your foot raised slightly off the ground behind you, bent knee forward (Illus. 30). Brush front, then brush back, ending in starting position (Illus. 31).

You have just done one shuffle. Try it with the other foot.

Now do three shuffles with one foot and step together, then do three shuffles with the other foot and step together. This time you will count in double time. Since a shuffle has two sounds, one sound will get a number (brush front) and the second sound will get an "and" (brush back).

Three shuffles and step-together combination:

Right foot	Shuffle (brush front, brush back)	
		1& (and)
	Shuffle	2&
	Shuffle	3&
	Step together	4
Left foot	Shuffle	5&
	Shuffle	6&
	Shuffle	7&
	Step together	8

Repeat the above exercise four times.

Illus. 30

Illus. 31

Illus. 32   **Illus. 33**

In tap a "step" refers only to stepping on the toe tap (Illus. 32).

Stepping on the entire foot is called a stamp (Illus. 33).

Step Heel

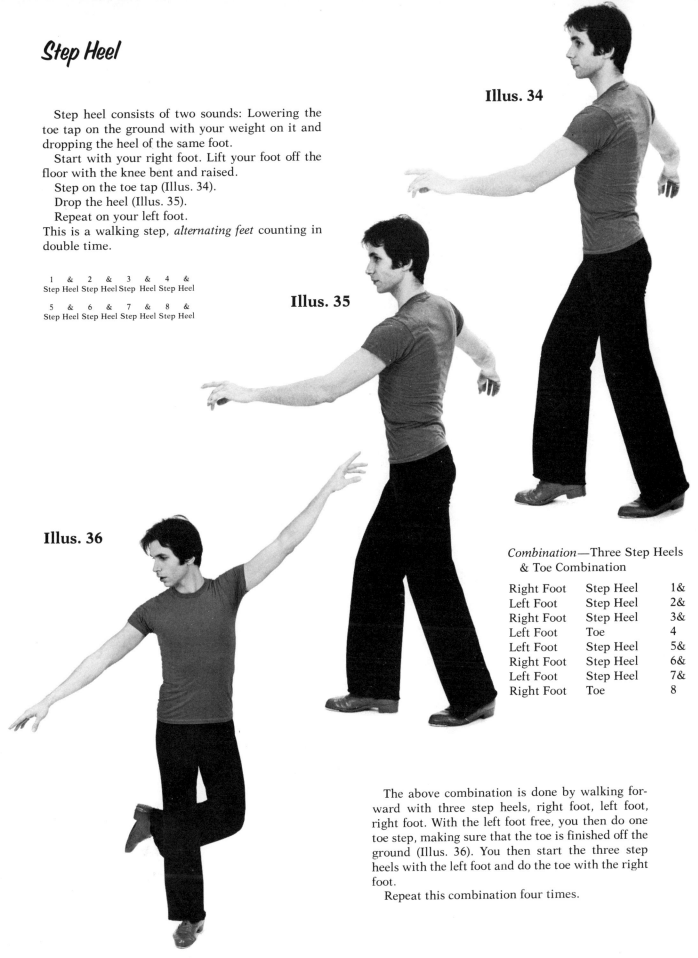

Step heel consists of two sounds: Lowering the toe tap on the ground with your weight on it and dropping the heel of the same foot.

Start with your right foot. Lift your foot off the floor with the knee bent and raised.

Step on the toe tap (Illus. 34).

Drop the heel (Illus. 35).

Repeat on your left foot.

This is a walking step, *alternating feet* counting in double time.

1 & 2 & 3 & 4 &
Step Heel Step Heel Step Heel Step Heel

5 & 6 & 7 & 8 &
Step Heel Step Heel Step Heel Step Heel

Illus. 34

Illus. 35

Illus. 36

Combination—Three Step Heels & Toe Combination

Right Foot	Step Heel	1&
Left Foot	Step Heel	2&
Right Foot	Step Heel	3&
Left Foot	Toe	4
Left Foot	Step Heel	5&
Right Foot	Step Heel	6&
Left Foot	Step Heel	7&
Right Foot	Toe	8

The above combination is done by walking forward with three step heels, right foot, left foot, right foot. With the left foot free, you then do one toe step, making sure that the toe is finished off the ground (Illus. 36). You then start the three step heels with the left foot and do the toe with the right foot.

Repeat this combination four times.

Illus. 37

Lesson Two

Tapping Forward Ending with the Heel

Start by repeating the toe-tap combination.

Tapping forward ending with the heel

With your right foot back, toe pointing out and your weight on your left foot, swing your leg around to the front while tapping 7 times (making a half circle). (Illus. 38-41.)

Leaving your toe tap down on the seventh tap, transfer your weight to it, and drop your heel (Illus. 40 and 41).

You are now in position to begin with your left foot; swing your leg around to the front the same way and drop your heel.

Repeat this on both the right foot and the left.

Counting in Single Time

Right foot swings forward
Seven taps (1234567)
Heel drop (8)

Left foot swings forward
Seven taps (1234567)
Heel drop (8)

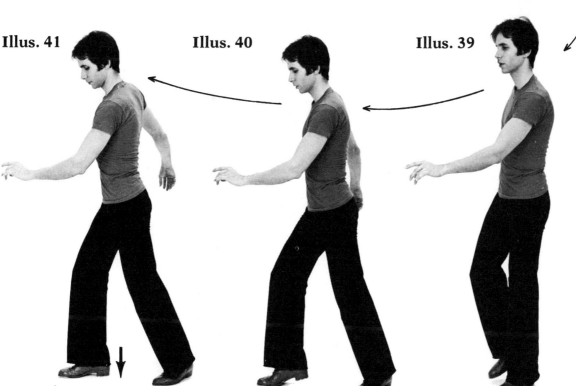

Illus. 38

Illus. 41   **Illus. 40**   **Illus. 39**

Illus. 42

Illus. 43

Illus. 44

Illus. 45

Tapping Backward with Heel

To reverse this step begin with the right foot forward, weight on your left foot (Illus. 42). Making a half circle, swing your leg around to the back while tapping seven times (Illus. 42-44) ending as in Illus. 44.

Leaving your toe tap down on the seventh tap, transfer your weight to it and drop your heel (Illus. 45).

You are now in position to begin the left foot: swing your leg around to the back while tapping the floor seven times, transfer your weight to the seventh tap, and drop your heel.

Repeat this on the right foot and the left foot. Count in the same pattern as tapping forward, ending with the heel.

Now quickly, bring your right leg straight through to the back, keeping your weight on the left foot. Combine:

As right foot swings forward—tap seven times and drop heel.

As left foot swings forward—tap seven times and drop heel.

As right foot swings forward—tap seven times and drop heel.

As left foot swings forward—tap seven times and drop heel.

Now, quickly bring right leg to the front (Illus. 46), repeat the above sequence swinging the leg around to the back.

This step is executed in eight straight sets of eight counts, four sets moving forward and four sets moving backwards.

Illus. 46

Illus. 47

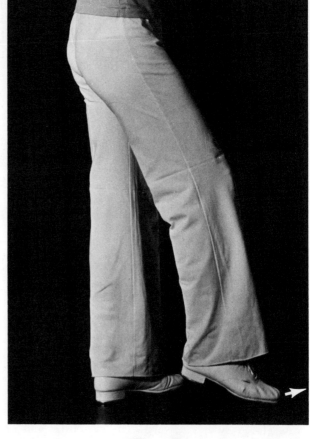

Illus. 48

Flap without Weight on the Working Foot

This step consists of two sounds: a brush forward and a touch (tap with no weight) made with the ball of the foot.

Weight on your left foot (hold onto a chair if necessary), brush front with your right foot (Illus. 47), straightening your leg (Illus. 48 and 49). Touch the floor with your right toe tap with foot pointed (Illus. 50).

Bring foot back to starting position and repeat.

Do eight flaps on your right foot.

Do eight flaps on your left foot.

Illus. 49   **Illus. 50**

This is counted in double time:

The brush gets the "and" count, the touch gets the number count.

Flap (brush-touch)	&1	(&5)
Bring foot back to starting position	&2	(&6)
Flap	&3	(&7)
Bring foot back to starting position	&4	(&8)

Continue this pattern for eight flaps on the right foot and eight flaps on the left foot.

Repeat the three shuffles and step-together combination from Lesson One.

Toe Dig Step Together

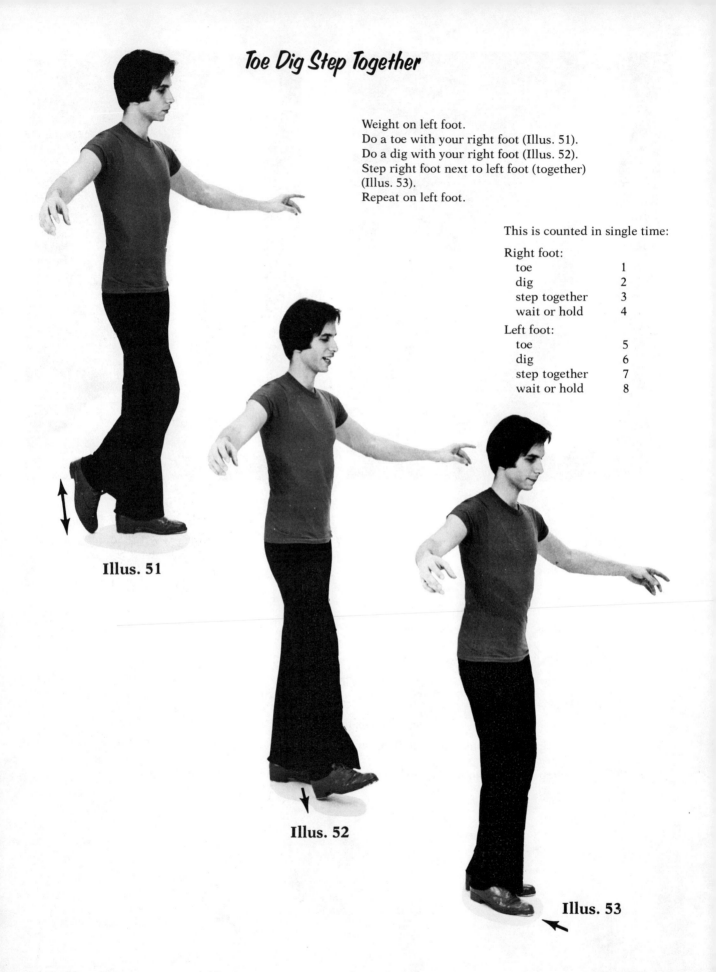

Weight on left foot.
Do a toe with your right foot (Illus. 51).
Do a dig with your right foot (Illus. 52).
Step right foot next to left foot (together)
(Illus. 53).
Repeat on left foot.

This is counted in single time:

Right foot:

toe	1
dig	2
step together	3
wait or hold	4

Left foot:

toe	5
dig	6
step together	7
wait or hold	8

Illus. 51

Illus. 52

Illus. 53

Ball Change

1. Two sounds are made by stepping on the ball of one foot with your weight on it, and jumping to the ball of your other foot, transferring your weight to it.

2. Start with your right leg in back (holding onto a chair, if necessary). Step on the ball of your right foot, lifting your left foot off the ground, knees bent slightly (Illus. 54).

3. Step to the ball of your left foot (keeping your right foot in back) and lift your right foot off the floor, knees bent slightly (Illus. 55).

4. Keep repeating this: step back, step front, back, front, back, front.

5. Now do it with your right foot front and left foot back.

6. To maintain your balance hold your stomach in and lean forward, even when you step back.

Illus. 54

Illus. 55

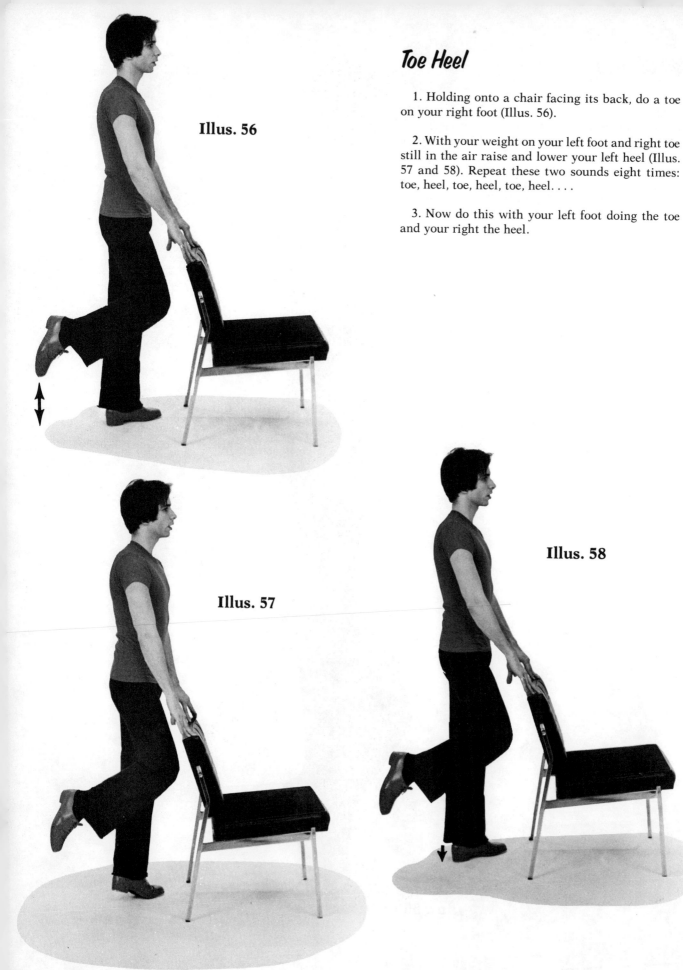

Toe Heel

1. Holding onto a chair facing its back, do a toe on your right foot (Illus. 56).

2. With your weight on your left foot and right toe still in the air raise and lower your left heel (Illus. 57 and 58). Repeat these two sounds eight times: toe, heel, toe, heel, toe, heel. . . .

3. Now do this with your left foot doing the toe and your right the heel.

Illus. 56

Illus. 57

Illus. 58

Illus. 59

Illus. 60

Lesson Three

Repeat the toe taps in Lesson One. Repeat seven taps ending on heel (four forward on each foot and four back on each foot). Do eight flaps front with your right foot. Do eight flaps front with your left foot.

Flap (Brush, touch)

As you become more proficient at doing flaps, you may try to execute the brush and touch in one motion. You can accomplish this by finishing the brush only slightly off the ground (Illus. 61-63) and immediately pointing your toe to do the touch (Illus. 64).

This will result in the sounds coming out one immediately after the other.

Illus. 61

Illus. 62

Illus. 63

Illus. 64

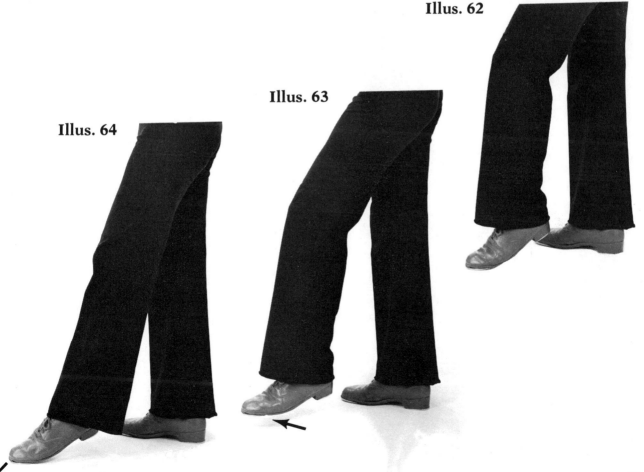

Shuffles

Repeat the three shuffles and step-together combination from Lesson One.

Try to do it a little faster than you have done it before. In dance, speeding the pace of a step is also referred to as quickening the *tempo*.

In the previous combination you were doing your shuffles to the front. Now you will do the same combination shuffling to the side instead of front.

Begin with your weight on your left foot. Lift your right foot off the floor slightly behind you. Now, turn your right knee out to the side (Illus. 65). The knee should be pointing out diagonally (in-between directly front and directly side).

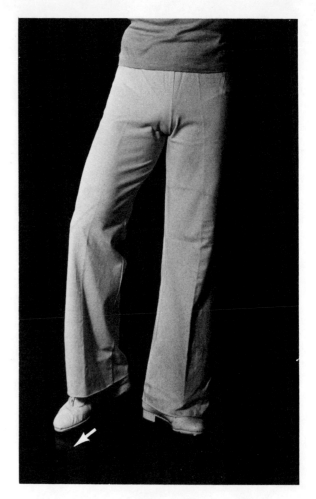

Illus. 66

Illus. 65

Do one shuffle out in the direction where your knee is pointed—brush front, brush back. (Illus. 66-69.)

Remember try only to use that part of your leg from the knee down.

Try the same side shuffle step-together combination, shuffling only to the side.

Do the entire combination four times (right foot and left foot).

Illus. 67

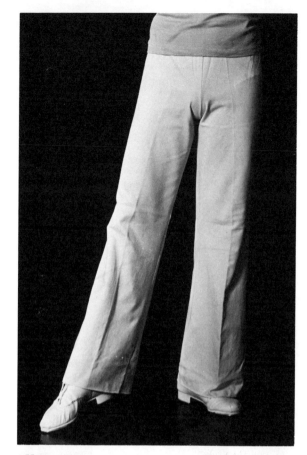

Illus. 68

Illus. 69

Toe Heel Step-Together Combination

1. Do a toe with your right foot (Illus. 70) and drop your left heel as in Lesson Two (Illus. 71). (No chair this time.)

2. Step right foot down next to left (together) (Illus. 72).

3. Now do a toe with your left foot and drop your right heel with weight as in Lesson Two.

4. Step together.

5. Remember a "toe" finishes in the air, not on the floor. You must bounce the tip of the tap off the floor as though the floor was red hot.

6. Alternate right foot then left foot each time. Do the entire combination (right foot and left foot) four times.

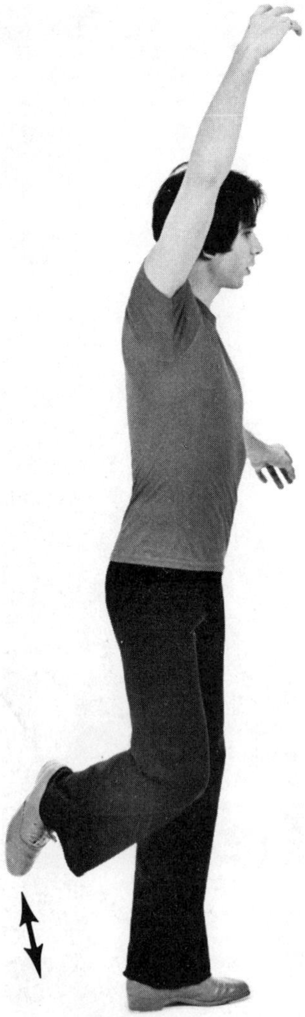

Illus. 70

Illus. 71

Illus. 72

Right	Toe	1
Left	Heel	2
Right	Step	3
	Hold	4
Left	Toe	5
Right	Heel	6
Left	Step	7
	Hold	8

Shuffle-Ball Change

Combine the shuffle with the ball change you
learned in the last lesson to make four sounds.

1. Shuffle your right foot (front shuffle) (Illus.
73-75). You should now be standing on your left
foot with your right foot raised off the floor slightly
behind you and knee bent (Illus. 75).

2. Step back on the ball of your right foot lifting
your left foot off the ground in front of you (Illus.
76).

Illus. 73

Illus. 76

Illus. 75

Illus. 74

3. Step on the ball of your left foot lifting your right foot off the floor in back of you. Your weight is now on the left foot and your right foot is free in position to do another shuffle-ball change (Illus. 77).

Repeat shuffle-ball change seven times on your right foot counting in single time.

Remember that the shuffle finishes with your foot up in the back and you step down in back on that foot.

You may use a chair to hold onto. If you do, remember that your heels stay off the floor throughout this exercise.

Shuffle-Ball Change	Brush front	1
	Brush back	2
	Ball of one foot	3
	Ball of other foot	4

Reverse this step, shuffle your left foot, step back on the ball of your left foot, and step to the ball of your right foot in front of you.

Do eight shuffle-ball changes with your left foot shuffling (no heels, please).

Illus. 77

Illus. 78

Combination

STEP HEEL on your Right Foot (Illus. 78, 79)
TOE on your Left Foot (Illus. 80)
STAMP on your Left Foot (Illus. 81)
STAMP on your Right Foot (Illus. 82)

Step Heel	1&
Toe	2 (hold &)
Stamp	3 (hold &)
Stamp	4

Now, reverse and start on your left foot.

Step Heel	Left	5&
Toe	Right	6(&)
Stamp	Right	7(&)
Stamp	Left	8

Do the entire combination (starting on right foot, then on left foot) eight times.

Illus. 79

Illus. 80

Illus. 81

Illus. 82

Illus. 83

Lesson Four

Repeat toe-taps combination (*en croix*).
Repeat seven taps ending in heel combination.
    Four sets forward on each foot.
    Four sets back on each foot.
Repeat three shuffles and step-together combination.
Repeat three step-heels and toe combination.

Flaps Side

1. Begin with your weight on your left foot. Lift your right foot off the floor slightly behind you. Now turn your right knee out to the side (Illus. 84). The knee should be pointing out diagonally (in between directly front and directly side).

2. Do one flap in the direction where your knee is pointing (brush-touch) (Illus. 85-87).

3. Try not to do the flap too far away from your body. Keep your balance (Illus. 86).

4. Bring your right foot back to the starting position.

5. Do eight side flaps with your right foot (&1, &2, &3, &4 . . .)

6. Do eight side flaps with your left foot (&1, &2, &3, &4 . . .).

Illus. 84

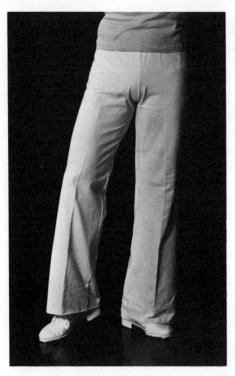

Illus. 85

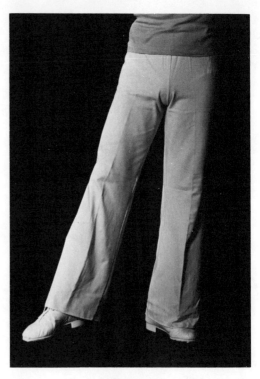

Illus. 86

Flaps Front-Side Combination

Weight on left foot then right foot:

Flap front	&1 wait &2
Flap side	&3 wait &4
Flap front	&5 wait &6
Flap side	&7 wait &8
Flap front	&1 wait &2
Flap side	&3 wait &4
Flap front	&5 wait &6
Step together	7 wait 8

Repeat the above pattern using your other foot.

Eight Shuffles Front and Side

1. Holding onto a chair at your left side with your left hand:

Do eight shuffles front with your right foot.

Do eight shuffles side with your right foot.

2. Repeat this pattern using your left foot. As you do these shuffles keep those two thoughts in mind.

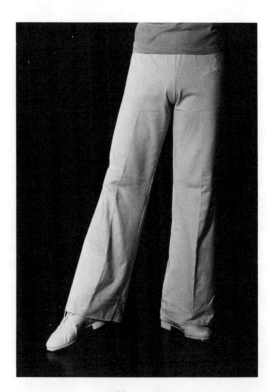

Illus. 87

Begin to make your leg movements smaller. Start with your feet a little closer to the ground and not so far behind you. Shuffle closer to your body (Illus. 88).

As you become more accustomed to doing these steps, you must try to use less leg action and more ankle action.

Think of that brush back as you quicken your shuffle. Accent it (make it a little louder than the brush front)—front back, front back, front back. . . .

Count: &1 &2 &3 &4 &5 &6 &7 &8.

Repeat the toe-heel step combination.

Illus. 88

Shuffle-Ball Change and Step-Together Combination:

1. Do three shuffle-ball changes with your right foot, shuffling.

2. After you have completed your third shuffle-ball change, your right foot is free.

3. Step your right foot down together.

4. Do three shuffle-ball changes on your left foot.

5. Step together.

Remember no heels on the shuffle-ball change so get way up on your toes.

Flap Heel:

Brush	&
Step	1
Heel	2

This is a walking step like the step heel but you substitute a flap for the step.

1. With your weight on your left foot, flap your right foot front keeping your knee bent (Illus. 89, 90). Transfer your weight to your right foot as you flap, leaning forward (Illus. 91).

2. Drop your right heel (Illus. 92).

3. With your weight now on your right foot, flap your left foot forward with your knee bent. Transfer your weight to your left foot as you flap. Drop your left heel.

4. Continue this pattern doing twelve flap heels. Count &1, 2, &3, 4, &5, 6, &7, 8. . . .

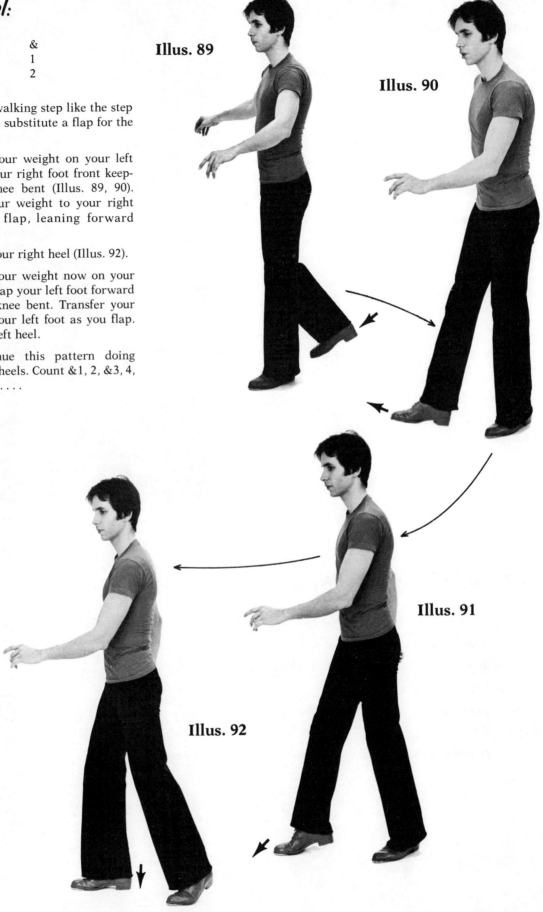

Illus. 89

Illus. 90

Illus. 91

Illus. 92

Shuffle-Toe-Dig-Stamp Combination:

With weight on your left foot:
1. Shuffle your right foot (Illus. 93). &1
2. Do a toe with your right foot (Illus. 94). 2
3. Do a dig with your right foot (Illus. 95). 3
4. Step your right foot together with your left. (Illus. 96). 4

Repeat using left foot   &5, 6, 7, 8

Do entire combination eight times.

Illus. 93   **Illus. 94**   **Illus. 95**   **Illus. 96**

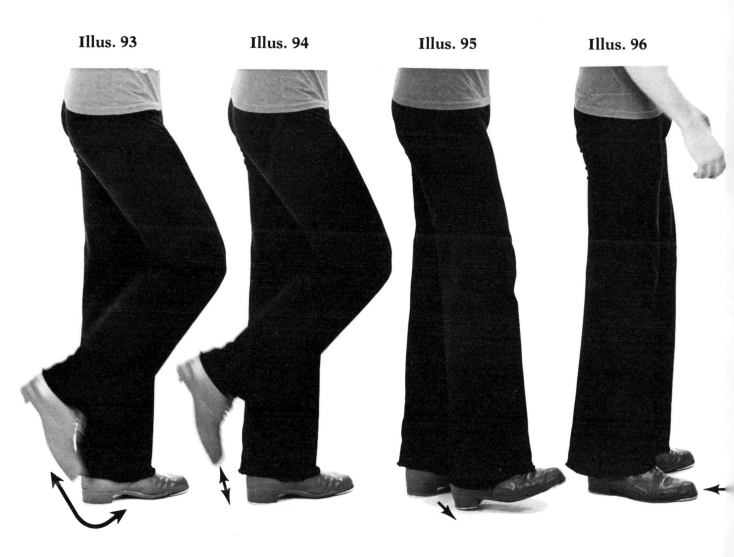

Illus. 97

Lesson Five

1. Repeat toe-tap combination.

2. Repeat seven taps and heel combination.

3. Repeat flaps front and side combination.

4. Eight shuffles front and side combination.

Substitute seven shuffles for the three shuffles in the three shuffles and step-together combination.

Holding a chair, if necessary, do

1. Seven front shuffles with your right foot and step together.

2. Seven front shuffles with your left foot and step together.

3. Seven shuffles to the side with your right foot and step together.

4. Seven shuffles to the side with your left foot and step together.

Count seven shuffles as &1 &2 &3 &4 &5 &6 &7
Step together   8

5. Do sixteen flap heels, alternating feet (flap heel with right foot, flap heel with left foot. . . .), walking forward.

Counts for flap heels are &1, 2, &3, 4, &5, 6, &7, 8.

Illus. 98

49

Cramp Rolls

Illus. 99

This step consists of four sounds made by stepping on one toe tap and then the other toe tap followed by dropping one heel and then the other heel. Four consecutive sounds: step, step, heel, heel.

With slightly bent knees step forward on your right toe-tap (Illus. 99) and then step on your left toe-tap (Illus. 100) bringing your feet together (heels off the ground).

Illus. 100

Drop your right heel (Illus. 101).

Then your left heel (Illus. 102).

You have just done one right cramp roll.

Do eight cramp rolls forward.

	Counts
Right Toe-Tap	1
Left Toe-Tap	2
Right Heel-Drop	3
Left Heel-Drop	4

Illus. 101

Illus. 102

Repeat this procedure stepping on your left toe-tap and then your right toe-tap. Drop your left heel and then your right heel. This is called a left cramp roll.

Do eight left cramp rolls.

Repeat shuffle-ball change and step-together combination.

Shuffle Step-Heel Combination

Knees bent, weight on your left foot

1. Shuffle your right foot to the side (Illus. 103).

2. Do a step heel in place with your right foot (Illus. 104, 105).

3. Knees bent, weight on your right foot, shuffle your left foot to the side and do a step heel in place with your left foot.

Shuffle right foot	1, 2
Step right foot	3
Heel right foot	4
Shuffle left foot	5, 6
Step left foot	7
Heel left foot	8

Repeat the above pattern four times (right foot and left foot).

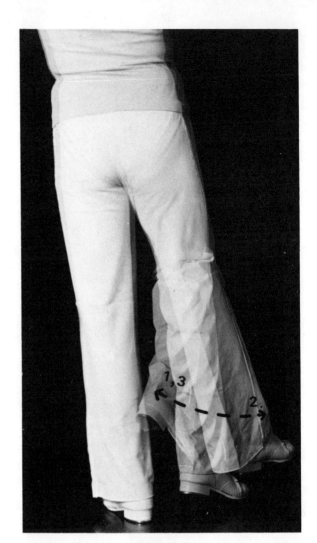

Illus. 103

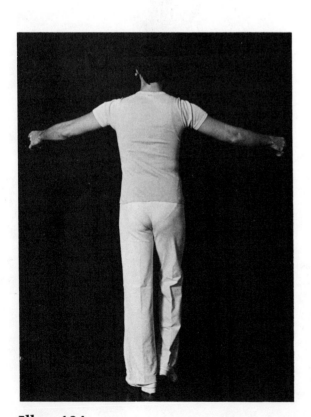

Illus. 104

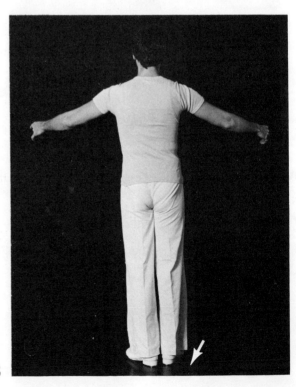

Illus. 105

Flap-Heel-Toe-Clap Combination

1. Do a flap heel with your right foot (Illus. 106, 107).

2. Do a "toe" with your left foot (Illus. 108). (Leave it on the floor.)

3. Clap (with your left foot still on the floor) (Illus. 109).

4. Flap heel with your left foot.

5. Do a "toe" with your right foot. (Leave it on the floor.)

6. Clap (with your right foot still on the floor).

Do the above pattern eight times.

Right flap	&1
Right heel	2
Left toe	3
Clap	4
Left flap	&5
Left heel	6
Right toe	7
Clap	8

Illus. 106

Illus. 107

Illus. 108

Illus. 109

Illus. 110

Lesson Six

Repeat toe-tap combination.
Repeat seven taps and heel combination.
Repeat flaps front and side combination.

Repeat seven shuffles front and side (and step together) combination.
Do eight right cramp rolls.
Do eight left cramp rolls.

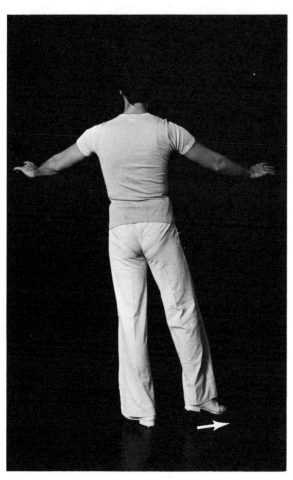

Flap to Side, Dropping-Standing Heel Combination:

1. Knees bent, weight on left foot, flap your right foot to the side (Illus. 110, 111).
2. Lift and drop your left heel in place with your weight on that left foot (Illus. 112, 113).
3. Bring your right foot in, step together (Illus. 114).
4. Knees bent, weight on right foot, flap your left foot to the side.
5. Lift and drop your right heel in place with your weight on that right foot.
6. Step together.

(Right foot)	Flap to side	&1
(Left foot)	Heel	2
(Right foot)	Step together	3
	Hold	4
(Left foot)	Flap to side	&5
(Right foot)	Heel	6
(Left foot)	Step together	7
	Hold	8

Repeat the above pattern 4 times.

Illus. 111

Illus. 112

Illus. 113

Illus. 114

Shuffle-Step Combination

1. With your knees slightly bent, stand on your toes (Illus. 115).
2. Shuffle your left foot to the side (Illus. 116-118).
3. Step in on the ball of your left foot (together) (Illus. 119).
4. Shuffle your right foot the same way.
5. Step on the ball of your right foot (together).
   You may want to hold onto the back of a chair.

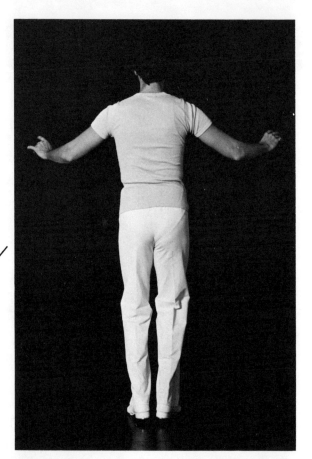

Illus. 115

Illus. 116

Illus. 117

Illus. 118

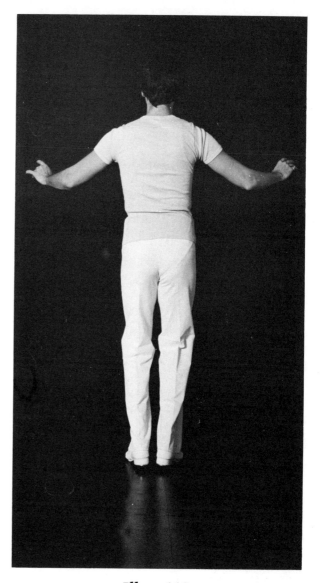

Do not accent the brush back.

Count in single time, tapping all sounds evenly.

Right foot	Brush front	1
	Brush back	2
	Step together	3
	Hold	4
Left foot	Brush front	5
	Brush back	6
	Step together	7
	Hold	8

Illus. 119

Repeat this pattern 8 times
  • Hold your stomach muscles up and in.
  • Hold on to the chair lightly, just resting your fingertips on it.

Flap-Ball Change

This is a travelling step done entirely on the balls of the feet. We will take it at a walking pace for now. As you begin to feel more comfortable with the step, you may quicken the pace.

1. FLAP your right foot to the front (diagonally) transferring your weight to that foot (Illus. 120).

2. BALL CHANGE from your left foot to your right foot by stepping with your left foot up to your right (weight now on left foot) (Illus. 121).

3. . . . and stepping out on your right foot (weight on right foot) (Illus. 122).

You are now ready to do a flap-ball change to your left.

1. FLAP your left foot to the front (diagonally), transferring your weight to that foot.

2. BALL CHANGE from your right foot to your left foot by stepping with your right foot up to your left foot (weight now on right foot)

3. . . . and stepping out on your left foot (weight on left foot)

You are now in position to repeat the step again to the right by flapping your right foot.

The best way to imagine this type of ball change is to picture the way young children gallop: The back foot coming forward to meet the front foot and the front foot stepping out to the front (Illus. 123-125).

Right foot	Flap	&1
Left	Ball	&
Right	Change	2
Left	Flap	&3
Right	Ball	&
Left	Change	4

Repeat the pattern above 4 times (right foot and left foot)

Illus. 120	**Illus. 121**	**Illus. 122**

Illus. 123

Illus. 124

Do 8 flap-ball changes, travel forward

1. Count the flap-ball changes in double time (&1&2&3&4. . . .)

2. Try to accent the tap sound that falls on the NUMBER (not the "and"):

    the second sound of the flap (step)
    the second sound of the ball change

brush-STEP-ball-CHANGE,
   &   1   &   2

brush-STEP-ball-CHANGE. . . .
   &   3   &   4

Illus. 125

Illus. 126

Lesson Seven

Repeat toe-tap combination.
Repeat 7 taps ending in heel combination.
Repeat 7 shuffles front and side combination.
Repeat flaps front and side combination.
Do 8 right cramp rolls.
Do 8 left cramp rolls.

Shuffling to the Back

To shuffle to the back, stand with knees slightly bent and feet together, holding on to a chair if necessary.

1. With your weight on your right foot, lift your left foot off the floor and extend your left leg directly behind you, knee bent, toe pointing to the left (Illus. 127).

• Do not bring your leg too far behind you, keep your balance and keep a straight back.

• Try to keep your hips facing front. Do not twist them to the left. (You may bend your right knee to keep from twisting your hips).

2. Do 8 back shuffles trying to keep your leg motion (shuffling foot) to a minimum, but do not miss any sound (Illus. 128, 129).

Count: &1&2&3&4&5&6&7&8

Repeat, shuffling your right foot to the back.

Do 3 shuffle-ball changes, shuffling your right foot.

Step together.

Do 3 shuffle-ball changes, with your left foot shuffling. Step together.

1. Accent the second sound of the shuffle (brush back).

2. Accent the second sound of the ball change.

brush-BRUSH-ball-CHANGE,
&   1   &   2

brush-BRUSH-ball-CHANGE, . . .
&   3   &   4

Illus. 127

Now, do 7 shuffle-ball changes and step together (both right foot and left foot).

• On the seventh shuffle-ball change (the one before you step together and begin with the other foot), count as follows:

. . . . brush-BRUSH-ball-CHANGE,
        &   5   &   6

step together, wait.
    7   8

Repeat shuffle-step-heel combination.

Repeat shuffle-step combination.

Illus. 128

Illus. 129

Hop

Illus. 130

With knees bent, and your weight on your right foot, lift your left foot off the floor. Jump (hop) from the ball of your right foot and land on that same foot in place. (No heels, please) (Illus. 130).

Do 4 hops and repeat hopping on the ball of your left foot.

Shuffle-Hop-Step Combination

Illus. 131

Illus. 132

With knees bent, weight on your right foot, and leaning slightly forward

1. Shuffle your left foot (Illus. 131).
2. Hop on your right foot (left foot still in the air) (Illus. 132).
3. Step down on your left foot, transferring your weight to that foot (Illus. 133).
4. Shuffle your right foot.
5. Hop on your left foot.
6. Step down on your right foot, transferring your weight to that foot.

• Ideally, this combination should be done totally off your heels. You may try this while holding onto a chair.

• As you do the brush back (second sound of the shuffle) raise your knee to go into the hop.

• Do not accent the shuffle. Count evenly 1,2,3,4.

Right	Brush front	1
Right	Brush back	2
Left	Hop	3
Right	Step together	4
Left	Brush front	5
Left	Brush back	6
Right	Hop	7
Left	Step together	8

Illus. 133

Repeat the above pattern 8 times (both right and left feet).

Repeat the flap-heel-toe-clap combination.

Flap-Ball-Change-Toe-Step Combination

1. Do 2 flap-ball changes, beginning with the right foot, then the left, finishing with your right foot free, off the floor.

2. Do 1 "toe" with your right foot.

3. Step together.

4. Do one "toe" with your left foot.

5. Step together.

6. Repeat the entire combination, beginning again with your right foot.

Right foot	Flap	&1
Left-right	Ball change	&2
Left	Flap	&3
Right-left	Ball change	&4
Right	Toe	5
Left	Step together	6
Left	Toe	7
Right	Step together	8

Repeat the above pattern 4 times.

Illus. 134

Lesson Eight

Repeat 7 taps ending with heel combination.
Repeat flap front-and-side combination.
Repeat 7 shuffles front-and-side combination.
Repeat 7 shuffle-ball change combination.
Repeat flaps to side dropping standing-heel combination.
Try the shuffle-step combination without holding onto the chair.

Cramp Rolls to Side

Start with knees bent, leaning slightly forward.

1. Step out to your right on the ball of your right foot (Illus. 135).

2. Bring your left foot to your right foot, stepping together on the ball of your left foot (Illus. 136).

3. Drop your right heel, then your left heel (Illus. 137, 138).

Do 8 right cramp rolls to the side.

1. Step out to your left on the ball of your left foot.

2. Bring your right foot out to your left, stepping together on the ball of your left foot.

3. Drop your left heel, then your right heel.

Remember to keep your knees bent throughout.

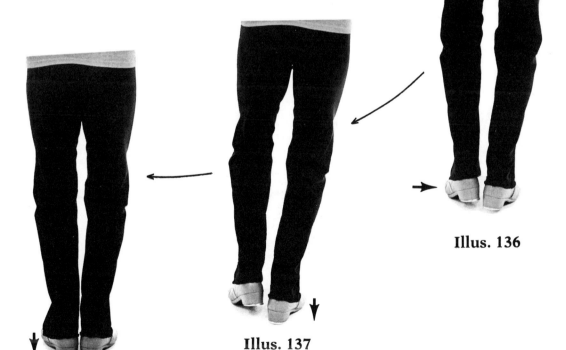

Illus. 135

Illus. 136

Illus. 137

Illus. 138

Running Flaps

Begin to learn this step by just walking on the balls of your feet, with your knees bent and your body leaning slightly forward.

Just relax your body and walk around the room, hearing your toe tap every time you step. Take small steps as in Illus. 139.

Do this for about a minute.

Now, with your knees bent and your weight on your left foot:

1. Brush your right foot front and step on the ball of the foot transferring your weight to it. (Illus. 140, 141.)

2. Brush your left foot front and step on the ball of your foot, transferring your weight to it.

Continue this pattern of walking flaps:

brush-step, brush-step, brush-step. . . .

Be sure to take small steps.
To get the feeling of running flaps, you must push off from one foot to the other as you flap.

These *small* jumps should look like Illus. 142. Leaning forward, kick your feet up slightly in the back as though you were jumping rope.

This step is not that simple to grasp when first learning it. Keep practicing running flaps, trying to make your steps and foot action smaller and smaller. As your steps improve from practicing, your sounds will become sharper.

At this point you are about halfway through the course. How does it feel? By now, you should have memorized the basic steps from Lessons One and Two. With a brief review, the other combinations (flap-ball change, shuffle-ball change, shuffle-step, etc.) should also seem more familiar upon execution. Both your balance and your grace should have improved with each lesson.

Illus. 139

Feel free to go at your own pace. Refer to earlier lessons to brush up or to clarify any questions about the steps or combinations that follow.

Illus. 140

Illus. 141

Illus. 142

Illus. 143

Lesson Nine

Repeat 7 taps ending in heel combination.
Repeat flaps front-and-side combination.
Repeat 7 shuffles front-and-side combination.
Repeat 7 shuffle-ball changes combination.
Repeat flaps to side dropping standing combination.
Repeat shuffle-step combination.
Repeat shuffle-hop-step combination.
Do 16 running flaps forward.
Do 8 cramp rolls to the right.
Do 8 cramp rolls to the left.
Do 16 flap heels walking forward.

With your knees bent, weight on your right foot:

1. Lift your left leg out to the side, left foot off the floor. (Illus. 144.)

2. Hop on the ball of your right foot 7 times gradually travelling to the right (only about a few inches at a time).

3. Step your left foot down.

4. Reverse the step, hopping 7 times on your left foot with your right foot off the floor.

5. Step your right foot down (together).

The hops are counts 1–7.
The step together is count 8.

Repeat the above pattern and remember: no heels touching the floor.

While you hop, hold your stomach in and up and try not to lift your shoulders.

Illus. 144

Combination

With your weight on your left foot:

1. Do one shuffle-ball change, shuffling your right foot. Your right foot is now free and off the floor (Illus. 145).

2. Flap your right foot to the right (diagonally), transferring your weight to that foot (Illus. 146).

3. Drop your right heel (Illus. 147). Your left foot is now free and off the floor.

4. Do one shuffle-ball change with your left foot. Your left foot is now free and off the floor.

5. Flap your left foot to the left (diagonally), transferring your weight to that foot.

6. Drop your left heel.

Now . . .

7. Hop 3 times on the ball of your right foot to the right.

8. Step together.

9. Hop 3 times on the ball of your left foot to the left.

10. Step together.

Illus. 145

Illus. 146

Illus. 147

Right foot	Shuffle	&1
Right-Left	Ball change	&2
Right	Flap	&3
Right	Heel	4
Left	Shuffle	&5
Left-Right	Ball change	&6
Left	Flap	&7
Left	Heel	8
Right	Hop, hop, hop	1 2 3
Left	Step together	4
Left	Hop, hop, hop	5 6 7
Right	Step together	8

1. Do the above pattern once.

2. Repeat it, reversing the feet.

3. In other words, begin by starting the shuffle-ball change with your left foot shuffling. Do the next shuffle-ball change with your right foot shuffling. Start your hops on your left foot and then on your right foot.

Illus. 148

Repeat 7 taps, ending in heel combination.
Repeat flaps to side dropping standing heel combination.
Repeat 7 shuffle-ball changes and step-together combination.
Do 16 flaps forward.
Do 8 right cramp rolls to the right.
Do 8 left cramp rolls to the left.

8 Shuffles en croix combination
With knees bent and your weight on the left foot:

Do 8 shuffles front	&1&2&3&4&5&6&7&8
Do 8 shuffles side	&1&2&3 . . .
Do 8 shuffles back	&1&2&3 . . .
Do 7 shuffles side	&1&2&3&4&5&6&7&
Step together	8

Repeat the above pattern shuffling your left foot.

Illus. 149

Waltz Clog

This step is danced to music in 3/4 time (Count 1,2,3,—4,5,6)
With your weight on your left foot:

1. Step out to your right on the ball of your right foot, transferring your weight to that foot (Illus. 148).

2. Shuffle your left foot to the side (Illus. 149, 150).

Illus. 150

Illus. 151

Illus. 152

Illus. 153

3. Step on the ball of your left foot (right foot lifted) (Illus. 151).

4. Step to the ball of the right foot. (left foot lifted) (Illus. 152).

You are now ready to begin this step with the left foot.

5. Step out to the left, transferring your weight to the ball of your left foot (Illus. 153).

6. Shuffle your right foot to the side.

7. Ball change from your right foot to your left foot, transferring your weight to the left foot (right foot lifted).

Count in double time

Right foot	Step	1	
Left	Shuffle	&2	Lean right
Left	Ball	&	
Right	Change	3	
Left	Step	4	
Right	Shuffle	&5	
Right	Ball	&	Lean left
Left	Change	6	

Repeat the above pattern (right foot and left foot) 8 times.

Remember to keep your heel off the floor.

As you do this step, lean towards the right for the 3 counts (waltz clog right), then lean to the left for the next three counts (waltz clog left). See pictures:

Buffaloes

Buffalo to the right

Begin with your weight on your left foot and right foot off the floor (Illus. 154).

1. Step out to the right on the ball of your right foot, lifting your left foot off the floor. Your left knee should be bent, ready to shuffle. (Illus. 155.)

2. Shuffle your left foot to the side (Illus. 156 and 157).

Illus. 154

Illus. 155

Illus. 156

3. Jump to the ball of your left foot (stepping directly in back of your right foot), lifting your right foot off the floor (Illus. 158).

Note in Illus. 158 that at the end of the step (when you jump to your left foot), the right foot lifts up *in front* of you. To repeat a buffalo you step out on the right foot from this position.

Right foot	Step	1	(5)
Left	Shuffle	&a	(&a)
Left	Jump	2	(6)
Right	Step	3	(7)
Left	Shuffle	&a	(&a)
Left	Jump	4	(8)

Repeat the above pattern 8 times (16 buffaloes).

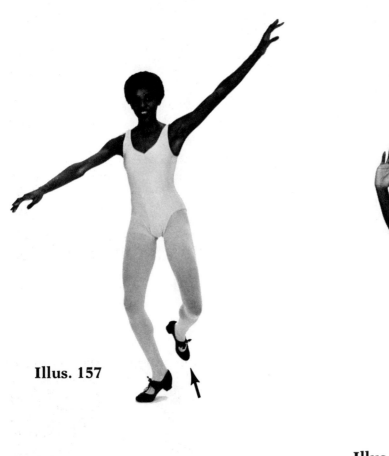

Illus. 157

Illus. 158

Buffaloes to the left
1. Step out to your left on the ball of your left foot (raising your right foot, knee bent).
2. Shuffle your right foot.
3. Jump to the ball of your right foot directly behind your left, lifting your left foot up in the front.
4. To repeat a buffalo, step out on the left foot from this position.

Do 16 buffaloes to the left.

Dig-Spank-Step-Heel Combination

Illus. 159

Illus. 160

Illus. 161

Begin with feet together, knees slightly bent:

1. Do a dig with your right foot (Illus. 159).

2. Brush your right foot back from the floor. (Illus. 160.) Do not lift your foot off the floor after the dig. Brush back from the dig position. This is known as a spank.

3. Step heel in place with your right foot (Illus. 161, 162).

Repeat the above pattern with your left foot.

	Dig	1
Right	Spank	2
	Step	3
	Heel	4
	Dig	5
Left	Spank	6
	Step	7
	Heel	8

Repeat this pattern 8 times (right and left foot alternating).

Illus. 162

Illus. 163

Lesson Eleven

Repeat 7 taps, ending in heel combination.
Repeat flaps to side dropping standing heel combination.
Repeat 8 shuffles *en croix*.
Repeat shuffle-step-heel combination. (Count &1 &2 . . .)
Do 16 flaps forward.
Do 8 left cramp rolls to the left.
Do 8 right cramp rolls to the right.
Do 8 buffaloes left.
Do 8 buffaloes right.

Double Shuffle

Stand on your right foot with your left knee pointing side, preparing to shuffle to the side (Illus. 164).

1. Do two quick shuffles (4 sounds) with your left foot (Illus. 165-167).

2. As you do these shuffles you must remember to make the minimum amount of movement with your shuffling foot (but still getting all the sounds).

Do not bring your foot too far off the ground (Illus. 167).

Try to accent only the last of the four sounds (the last brush).

Illus. 164

brush, brush, brush, BRUSH
  1   &   a   2
brush, brush, brush, BRUSH
  3   &   a   4

Do 8 double shuffles on your right foot
Do 8 double shuffles on your left foot

Illus. 165

Illus. 166

Illus. 167

Scuff

This is a sound made by striking your heel on the floor as your foot moves forward.

With your weight on your left foot and your right foot off the floor:

1. Scuff the floor with your right foot (Illus. 168-170).

Do 8 scuffs with your right foot.

Now with your weight on your right foot, do 8 scuffs with your left foot.

Combination

With your weight on your left foot:

1. Do one flap-ball change to the right beginning with your right foot. Your left foot should be free (off the floor).

Illus. 170

Illus. 169

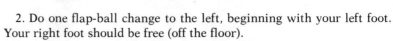

Illus. 168

2. Do one flap-ball change to the left, beginning with your left foot. Your right foot should be free (off the floor).

3. Do two right cramp rolls to the right.

Count in double time:

Right foot	Flap	&1
Left-right	Ball change	&2
Left	Flap	&3
Right-left	Ball change	&4
Right	Cramp roll	&5 &6
	(step-step-heel-heel)	
Right	Cramp roll	&7 &8

Now do the entire combination beginning with your left foot.

1. One flap-ball change to the left.
2. One flap-ball change to the right.
3. Two cramp rolls to the left.

Lesson Twelve

Repeat seven taps ending in heel.
Repeat flaps to side dropping standing heel combination.
Repeat eight shuffles *en croix*.
Repeat shuffle-hop-step combination. (Count &1 &2 &3 . . .)
Do 16 flaps forward.
Do the dig-spank-step-heel combination.
Do 8 double shuffles with your right foot.
Do 8 double shuffles with your left foot.

Step-Scuff-Hop Combination

Begin with your weight on your left foot and your right foot lifted off the floor.
1. Step on the ball of your right foot, transferring your weight to that foot (Illus. 171).
2. Scuff your left foot (Illus. 172).
3. Hop on the ball of your right foot (Illus. 173).

Now start with your left foot:
1. Step on the ball of your left foot, transferring your weight to that foot.
2. Scuff your right foot.
3. Hop on the ball of your left foot.

This step is done to music in 3/4 time.

Right foot	Step	1
Left	Scuff	2
Right	Hop	3
Left	Step	4
Right	Scuff	5
Left	Hop	6

Repeat the above pattern eight times.

Illus. 171

Illus. 172

Illus. 173

This is a walking step. Begin with your weight on your left foot.

1. Do a "toe" with your right foot (Illus. 174).
2. Scuff your right foot (Illus. 175).
3. Lift and drop your left heel (Illus. 176).
4. Do a "dig" with your right foot (Illus. 177).
5. Drop your right toe tap down to the floor (Illus. 178). From the dig position, do not lift your heel off the floor, but transfer your weight to the right foot.
6. Lift and drop your right heel (Illus. 179).

Continue with the left foot:

1. Do a "toe" with your left foot.
2. Scuff your left foot.
3. Drop your right heel.
4. Dig your left foot.
5. Drop your left toe tap down to the floor (do not lift your heel), transferring your weight to the left foot.
6. Lift and drop your left heel.

Do this step to music in 3/4 time:

Right	Toe	1		Left	Toe	1
Right	Scuff	2		Left	Scuff	2
Left	Heel	3		Right	Heel	3
Right	Dig	4		Left	Dig	4
Right	Step	5		Left	Step	5
Right	Heel	6		Left	Heel	6

Repeat this pattern 4 times.

Combination

With your weight on your left foot and your right foot lifted off the floor:

1. Do 4 running flaps forward, starting on your right foot (right, left, right, left).
Now that your right foot is free:
2. Do one shuffle-ball change, shuffling your right foot.
3. Stamp your right foot forward.

4. Clap.

Repeat the pattern, starting your flaps with your left foot:

1. 4 running flaps.
2. One shuffle-ball change, shuffling with your left foot.
3. Stamp forward with your left foot.
4. Clap.

Right foot	Flap	—	&1	—	Left Foot	Flap
Left	Flap	—	&2	—	Right	Flap
Right	Flap	—	&3	—	Left	Flap
Left	Flap	—	&4	—	Right	Flap
Right	Shuffle	—	&5	—	Left	Shuffle
Right-left	Ball change	—	&6	—	Left-right	Ball change
Right	Stamp	—	7	—	Left	Stamp
	Clap	—	8	—		Clap

Do the above combination 4 times.

Illus. 174   Illus. 175   Illus. 176

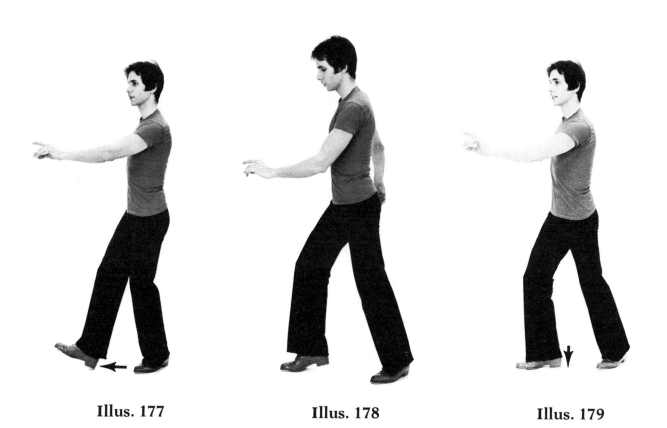

Illus. 177   Illus. 178   Illus. 179

Illus. 180

Lesson Thirteen

Repeat 7 taps, ending in heel combination.
Repeat flaps to side dropping standing heel.
Repeat 8 shuffles *en croix*.
Do 16 flaps forward.
Do 8 double shuffles with your right foot.
Do 8 double shuffles with your left foot.
Repeat the toe-heel-step combination.
Repeat shuffle-step combination. (Count &a1, &a2 . . .)
Repeat hop combination.

Shuffle Cramp Roll to the Right and Left

With your weight on your left foot:

1. Shuffle your right foot to the side (Illus. 180-182).

2. Pushing off your left foot, jump out to the right (about a foot), and land on the ball of your right foot (Illus. 183).

3. Bring your left foot next to your right foot and step on the ball of your left foot (Illus. 184).

4. Drop your right heel.

5. Drop your left heel.

Do 8 right shuffle cramp rolls.

With your weight on your right foot:

1. Shuffle your left foot to the side.

2. Pushing off your right foot, jump out to the left (about a foot), and land on the ball of your left foot.

Illus. 181

Illus. 182

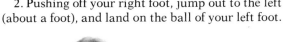

Illus. 183

Illus. 184

3. Bring your right foot next to your left and step on the ball of your right foot.

4. Drop your left heel.

5. Drop your right heel.

Do 8 shuffle cramp rolls to the left.

Illus. 185

Illus. 186

Illus. 187

Illus. 188

Waltz Clog-Step-Scuff-Hop Combination

Illus. 189

With your weight on your left foot:

1. Do a waltz clog starting with your right foot, then left foot.

Step on the ball of your right foot (Illus. 185).

Shuffle-ball change, shuffling your left foot.

Step on the ball of your left foot (Illus. 186).

Shuffle-ball change, shuffling your right foot.

Now with your right foot free:

2. Begin the step-scuff-hop combination, once, starting with your right foot and then with your left foot.

Step on the ball of your right foot (Illus. 187).

Scuff your left foot (Illus. 188).

Hop on the ball of your right foot (Illus 189).

Step on the ball of your left foot.

Scuff your right foot.

Hop on the ball of your left foot.

Your right foot is now free and ready to begin the waltz clog again.

This step is done in 3/4 time.

Right foot	Step	1
Left	Shuffle	&2
Left-right	Ball change	&3
Left	Step	4
Right	Shuffle	&5
Right-left	Ball change	&6
Right	Step	1
Left	Scuff	2
Right	Hop	3
Left	Step	4
Right	Scuff	5
Left	Hop	6

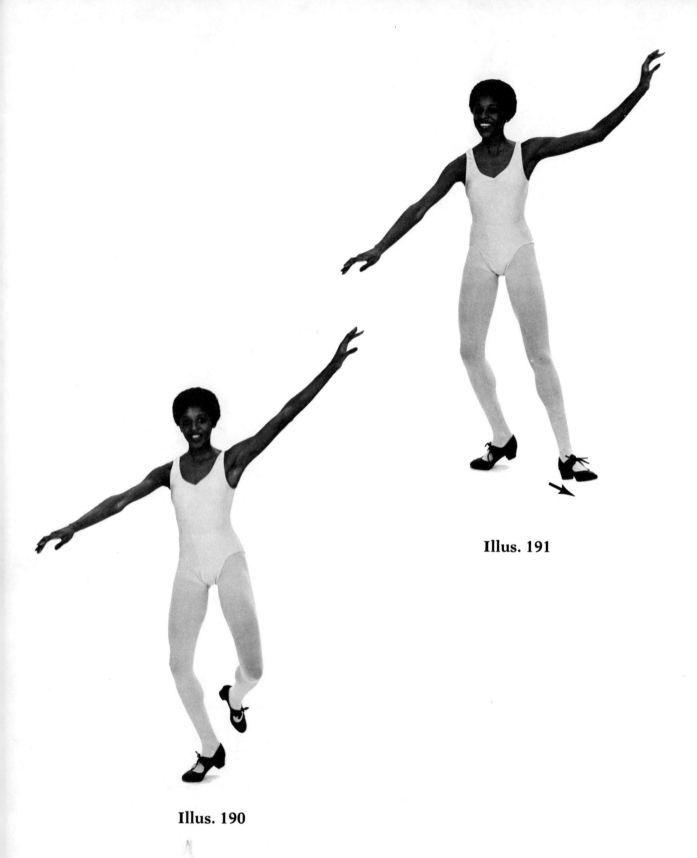

Illus. 191

Illus. 190

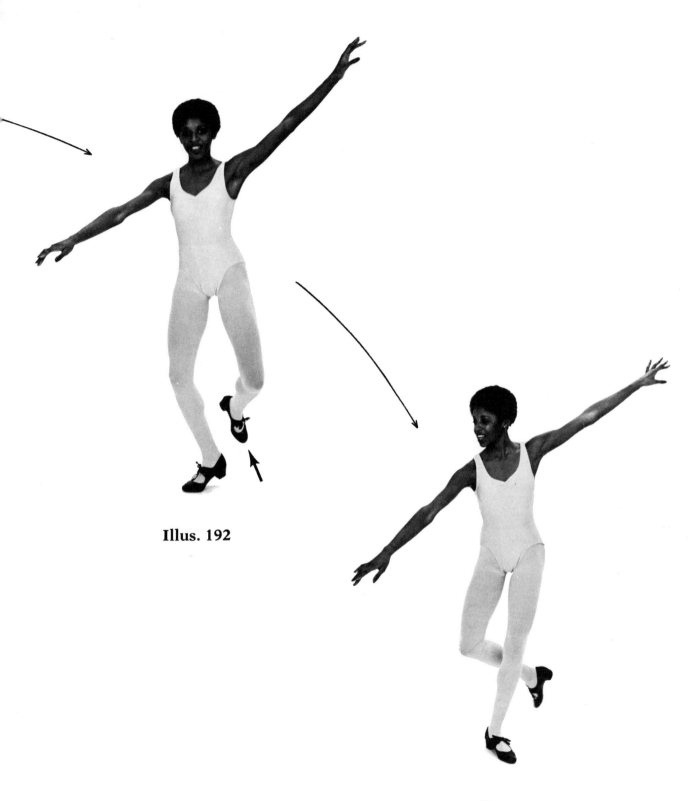

Illus. 192

Illus. 193

Lesson Fourteen

Repeat 7 taps ending in heel combination.
Repeat flaps to side dropping standing heel combination.
Repeat 8 shuffles *en croix*.
Repeat 7 shuffle-ball changes and step-together combinations.
Do 16 flaps forward.
Do 8 right shuffle cramp rolls.
Do 8 left shuffle cramp rolls.
Repeat the dig-spank-step-heel combination.

Illus. 194

Maxiford

Begin with knees bent, feet together:

1. Jump to the ball of your right foot, left foot off the floor (Illus. 190).

2. Shuffle your left foot to the side (Illus. 191, 192).

3. Jump to the ball of your left foot (underneath you) (Illus. 193).

4. Do a right "toe" crossing behind you (Illus. 194). Your right foot is free to repeat this combination.

Do 4 Maxifords, leaping to the right foot.

Begin with knees bent, feet together:

1. Jump to the ball of the left foot, right foot off the floor.

2. Shuffle your right foot to the side.

3. Jump to the ball of your right foot (underneath you).

4. Do a left "toe" crossing behind you.

5. Your left foot is now free to repeat this combination.

Do 4 maxifords, leaping to the left foot.

Do these steps to music in 3/4 time.

Jump (step)	1
Shuffle	&2
Jump	&
Toe	3
Jump	4
Shuffle	&5
Jump	&
Toe	6

Hop-Shuffle-Hop

Begin with your weight on your right foot and your left knee bent. (Left foot off the floor, prepared to shuffle—Illus. 195).

   1. Hop on the ball of your right foot (keep knee bent) (Illus. 196).

   2. Shuffle your left foot to the side.

   3. Hop again.

Illus. 195

Right foot	Hop	1
Left	Shuffle	&a
Right	Hop	2
Right	Hop	3
Left	Shuffle	&a
Right	Hop	4
Right	Hop	5
Left	Shuffle	&a
Right	Hop	6
Right	Hop	7
Left	Shuffle	&a
Right	Hop	8

Repeat this pattern hopping on your left foot and shuffling with your right foot.

Illus. 196

Illus. 197

Illus. 198

Illus. 199

Illus. 200

No matter what your age, you can begin tap dancing and have fun and exercise. (Above) Paula Martorano, has learned enough to put on a performance for friends and neighbors. (Left page) Carol Straker enjoys showing off her abilities including high kicking that only youngsters can do with ease.

Index